The
Wanderlust
Coloring Book

The
Wanderlust
Coloring Book

Take a trip around
the world with these
enticing images

SIRIUS

SIRIUS

This edition published in 2023 by Sirius Publishing, a division of
Arcturus Publishing Limited,
26/27 Bickels Yard, 151–153 Bermondsey Street,
London SE1 3HA

ISBN: 978-1-3988-3006-6
CH011157NT
Supplier 29, Date 0423, PI 00003261

Printed in China

Introduction

Whether you are a seasoned traveler who keeps a tally of the countries they have visited and thinks nothing of strapping on a backpack and venturing into the unknown, or a tourist of the armchair variety, this coloring book will provide plenty of inspiration for your travels, both actual and virtual.

You'll find iconic buildings from the world's great cities, such as the Eiffel Tower in Paris, the Colosseum in Rome, and San Francisco's Nob Hill mansions.

Or if you prefer to go more off the beaten track, there are desert scenes dotted with gigantic cacti, winding river valleys and mountain landscapes, including Japan's Mount Fuji. If you're a safari enthusiast or a scuba diver, there are images of the animals you'd see on such an adventure, including the dazzling creatures that inhabit a coral reef.

All you need to go on your travels is this book, a handful of colored pencils, and your favorite quiet spot and you're all set on a new adventure.

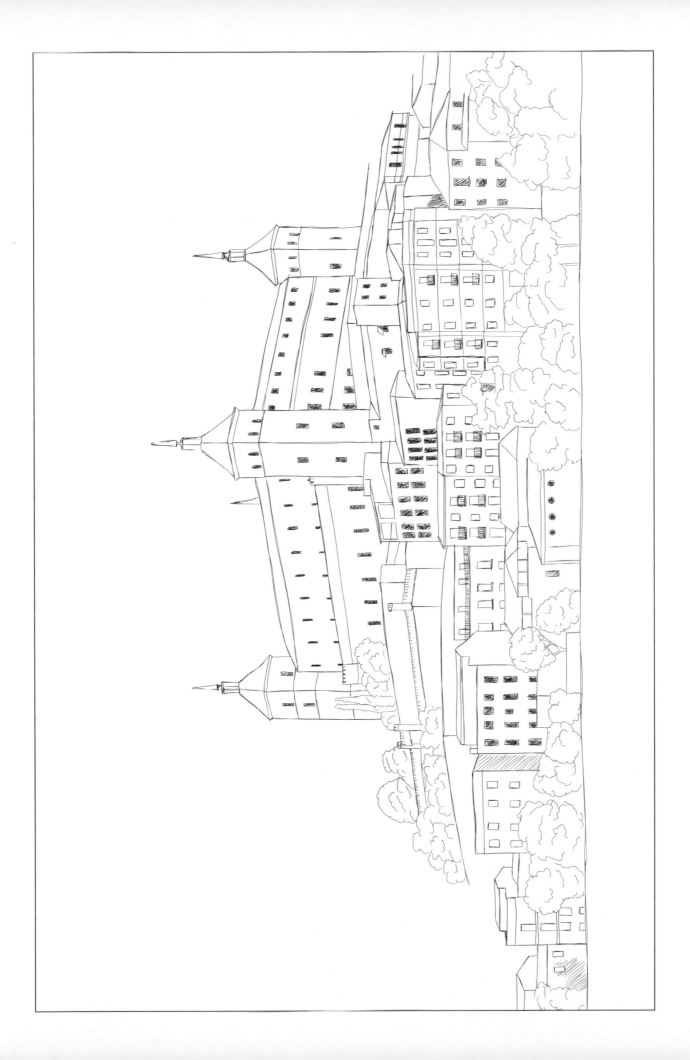

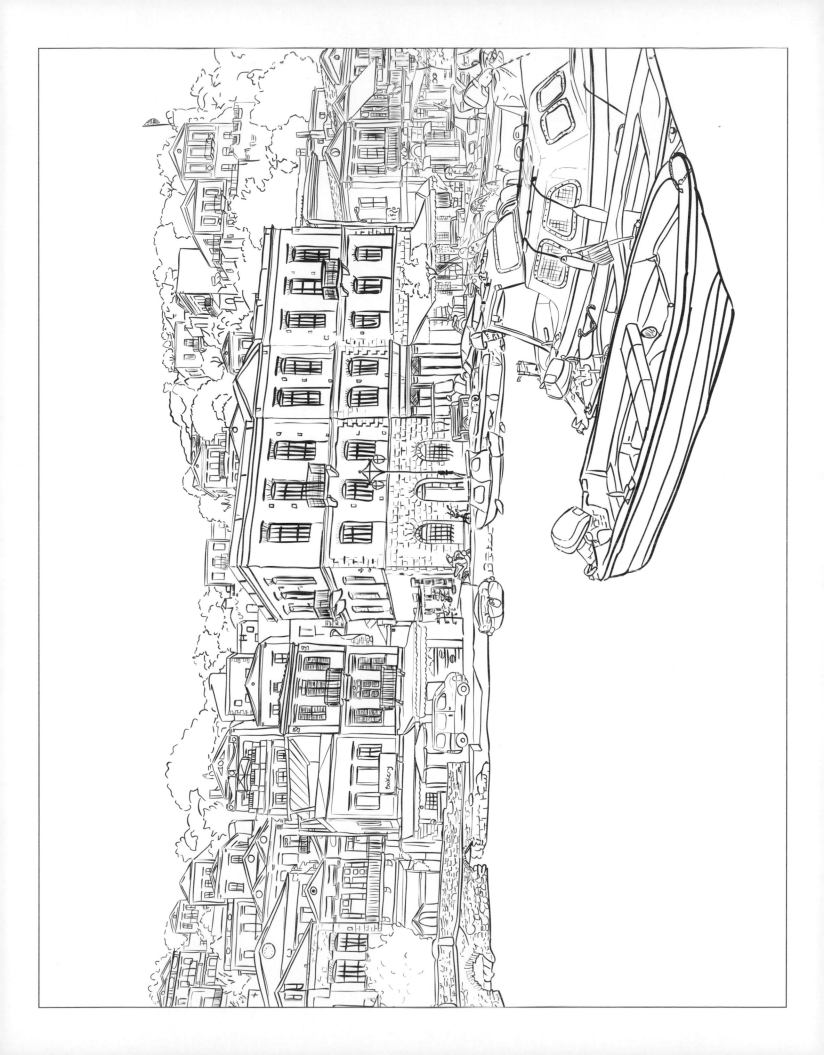

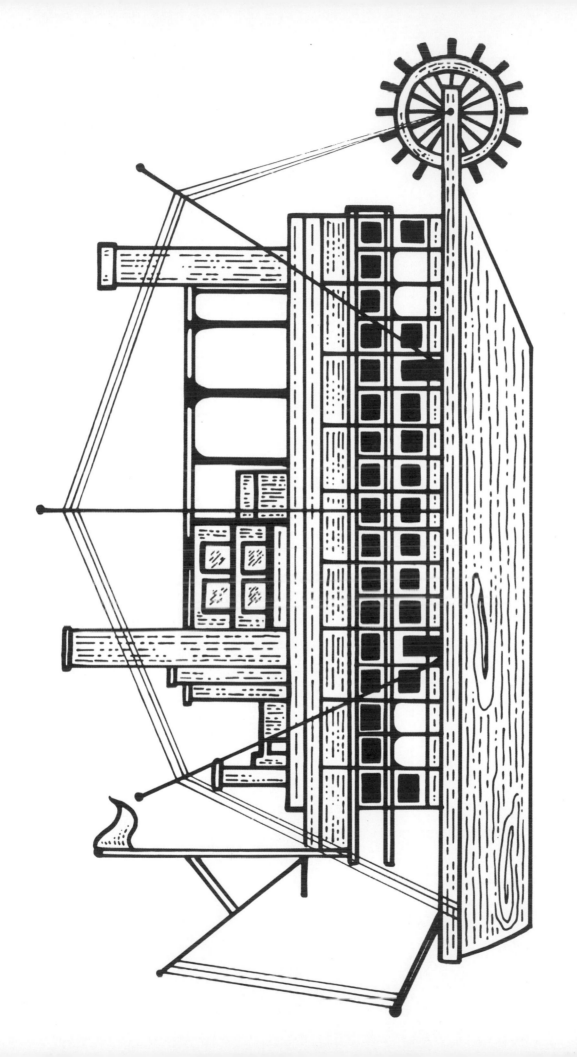

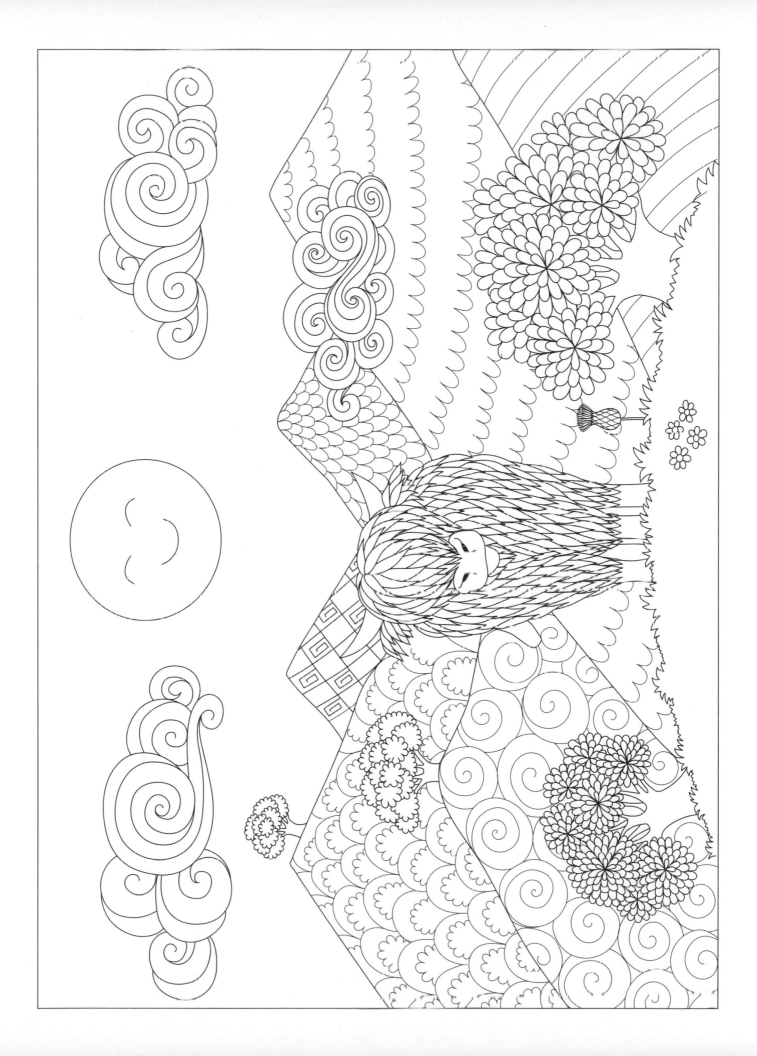

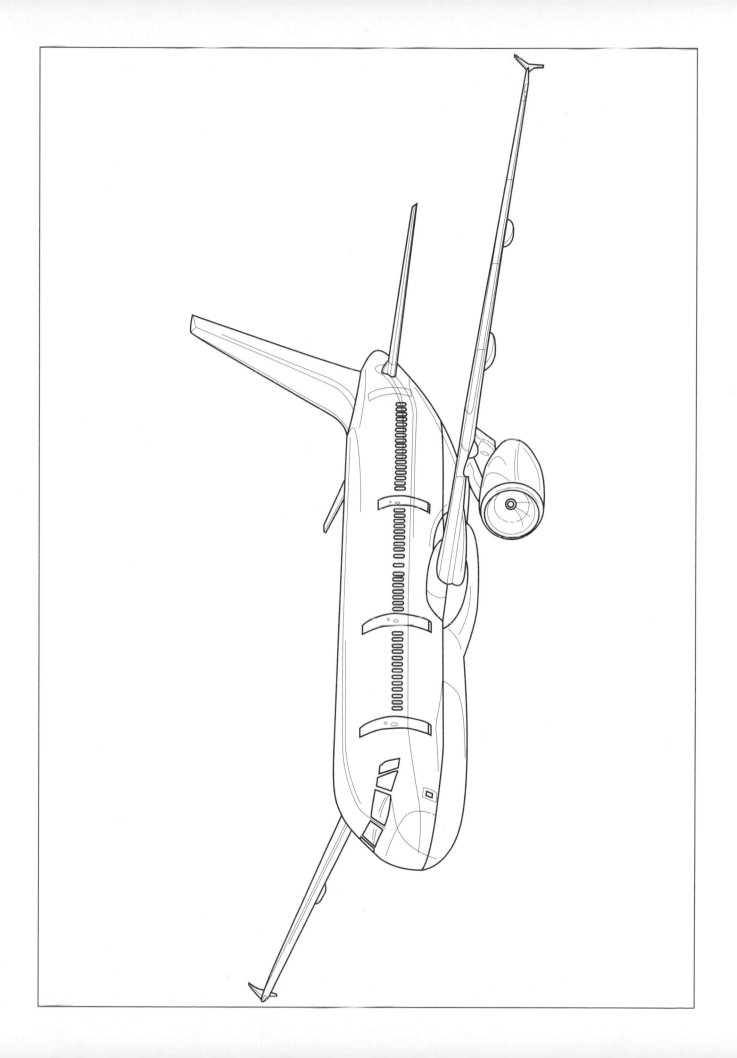

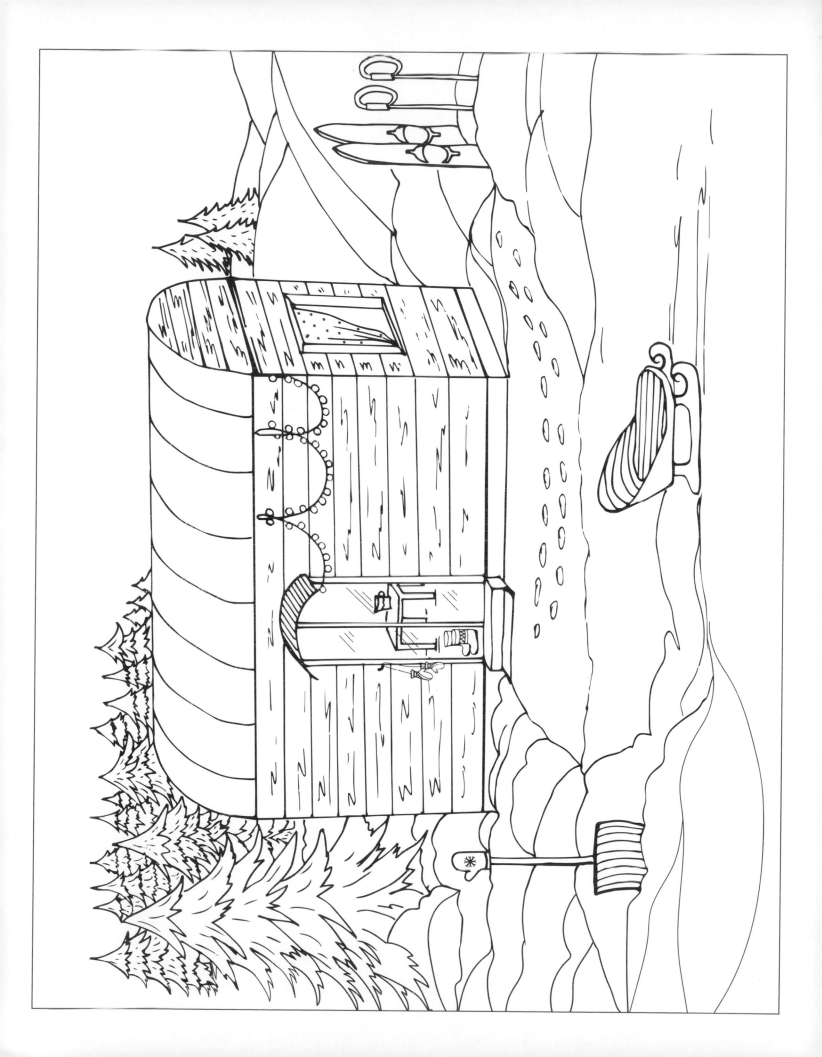

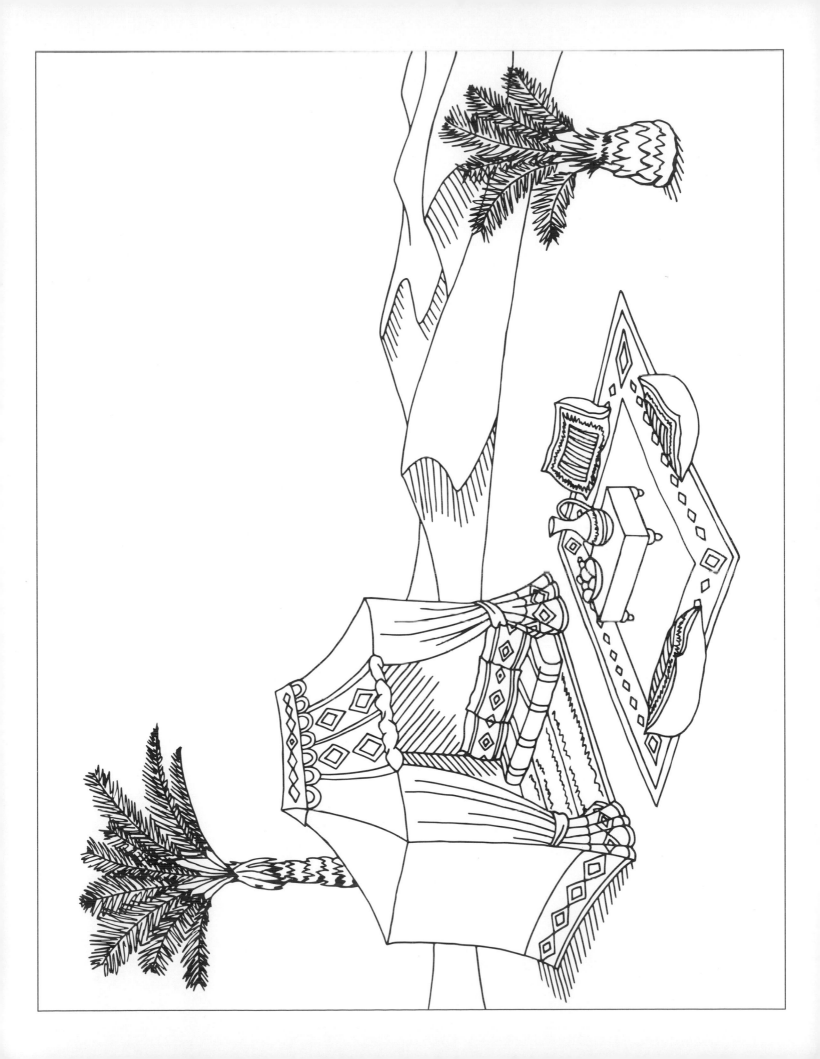